THIS IS ME!

ACROSTICS

Treasured Moments

Edited By Byron Tobolik

First published in Great Britain in 2022 by:

Young Writers — Est. 1991 —

Young Writers
Remus House
Coltsfoot Drive
Peterborough
PE2 9BF
Telephone: 01733 890066
Website: www.youngwriters.co.uk

Printed and bound in the UK by BookPrintingUK
Website: www.bookprintinguk.com
YB0509X

Foreword

Welcome Reader,

For Young Writers' latest competition *This Is Me Acrostics*, we asked primary school pupils to look inside themselves, to think about what makes them unique, and then write an acrostic poem about it! They rose to the challenge magnificently and the result is this fantastic collection of poems, celebrating them and the things that are important to them.

Here at Young Writers our aim is to encourage creativity in children and to inspire a love of the written word, so it's great to get such an amazing response, with some absolutely fantastic poems. It's important for children to focus on and celebrate themselves and this competition allowed them to write freely and honestly, celebrating what makes them great, expressing their hopes and fears, or simply writing about their favourite things. *This Is Me Acrostics* gave them the power of words.

I'd like to congratulate all the young poets in this anthology, I hope this inspires them to continue with their creative writing.

Contents

Evie Clewer (6) 71
Sivataruniya Piratheepan 72
Rejoice Agbaje (7) 73

Hunwick Primary School, Hunwick

Alfie Sanderson (7) 74
Masie Griffiths (6) 75
Beatrice Barker (7) 76
Sienna Blacklock (7) 77
Aimee Reidy (7) 78
Theo Cottrell (7) 79
Jessica Fielding (6) 80

Sherfield School, Sherfield-On-Loddon

Semih Quoi (9) 81

St Bride's Primary School, Bothwell

Brodie Miller (7) 83
Gabriella Canale (7) 84
Michael McCann (8) 85
Jack Reid (7) 86
Matthew Donnelly (7) 87
Michael McCallum (7) 88
Ezmay Dooley (7) 89
Alexander Farr (7) 90
Eilidh Scott (7) 91
James Reddin 92
Brooke McManus (7) 93
Lochlan Taggart (7) 94
Antonia Moraru (7) 95
Mia Craney (7) 96

Summerfield Primary School, Leeds

Lilly-Rose Holdsworth (7) 97
Casey (7) 98
Nathan Grabowski (6) 99
Poppy (6) 100
Travis Hannah (7) 101

Junior (7) 102

Topcliffe Primary School, Birmingham

Kasey Wilson (7) 103
Kyce Isaac-Witts (7) 104
Georgia Shearer (7) 105
Summer Hope (7) 106
Daisy Pritchard (7) 107
Noah Antcliff (7) 108
Katie-Rose Griffiths (8) 109
Jack Ancill-Durham (7) 110

Totternhoe CE Academy, Totternhoe

Harrison-J Odell (6) 111
Ethan Tingay (7) 112
Alden Rust (7) 113
Poppy Tebbutt (6) 114
Olivia Noble (6) 115
Ionatan Patrichi (6) 116
Martha Setterfield (7) 117
Otto Clarke (6) 118
Jessica Janes (6) 119
Joshua Law (6) 120
Harry Shuffleton (6) 121
David Frampton (7) 122
Rue Smith (6) 123
Bethany Phillips (5) 124
Charlie Chandler (6) 125
Oliver Mumford (5) 126
Evelyn Absalom (6) 127
Reggie Coppock (6) 128
Seren Low (5) 129
Taiya Douglas (6) 130
Caleb Derbidge (6) 131
Enzo Apollonio (6) 132
Luis Cox (6) 133

The
Acrostics

Growing Together

G row, grow! First, I was small, now I'm tall

R oll, roll and now I'm cold

O h, oh, oh, walk to the top

W orld, world, wow! I'm old

I 'm too old to crawl

N o, no, no, I'm old

G o, go, go, I'm too tall now

T ick-tock, I can hear the clock

O h, oh no, it's closed

G o, go, go away, this is my hiding space

E eeee! Witch alert!

T in, I love my tin

H ome, home, it's my home

E eeee! What's that noise?

R rrrr! Oh no, a monster!

Mohammad Samiullah Shakaib (7)

Poem About Seasons

W ind is howling and whirling
I n winter the air is freezing
N uts and animals would be hidden
T umbling snow is rocking through towns
E nchanting shapes of leaves dropping
R unning people are hovering

S pring is when the sky is full of bloom
P aradise animals and others are out of hibernation
R ising animals are ready for fun
I n spring the world is wonderful
N uts are having a reincarnation
G rass is showing off and shining green

A wonderful world where leaves change

U seless leaves but pretty leaves are changing

T ree leaves are looking great with a change of colour

U seless leaves but pretty leaves are changing

M ammals are hibernating from cold

N uts are collected by squirrels

S un is shining brightly

U seless people are sunbathing

M urmuring sounds from everywhere

M urmuring sounds from everywhere

E nchanting shades of sun are beaming

R ising animals are nibbling on fresh food.

Krishna Pritesh Vadolia (6)

Rose Le Mer Suresh

R ain is beautiful to me
O h, I really like Brittany
S eagulls stealing my ice cream - hmmph!
E at pancakes every day

L aughter - I like it!
E motions are good and bad

M y daddy - I love his curly hair!
E diting my work with green pens only
R eading long books on the sofa

S ea makes a beautiful sound, soft and sweet
U niform, blue, yellow and white - a swan
R unning, dancing and singing, those are my favourite things
E smée, Diana, Felix and Henry are my best friends

S chool is amazing because I like learning

H ooray, it's fun to do poems!

Rose Le Mer Suresh (5)

This Is Me!

P avan is my name
A sweet and caring girl
V ery intelligent and smart
A lways wanting to be perfect
N ever giving up on my dream of being a fashion designer

P ositive and full of joy
U nderstanding and hates to annoy
R eliable and very mature
E njoys to organise every drawer
W isdom is at the top of my list
A nd, of course, I'm a perfectionist
L oving, loyal and the kindest - has a fear of the sea. Now you know all about me!

Pavan Purewal (8)

A Treasure Trove Of This Is Me!

A T reasure trove of

H appiness is what I like to draw and see!

I magination is what I like to explore, like shells on a seashore

S elf-assured at being kind and being me, you see?

I nspired by sweet things: cookies, cats and cute dolls!

S eeker of secret messages and symbols, like a mole looking for light...

M y toy wonderland and music make me dance, swirl and sing

E xcited by eccentric videos and gaming worlds online that make my brain go zing!

Rosalind Thornhill-King (10)

My Favourite Dance Style Is Modern

M y favourite dance style is modern

O n stage is where I'm born to be!

D o you like the style, modern?

E arn a medal, you deserve it!

R eceive a trophy for doing so well

N ow you'll be a master modern dancer!

D o you want to dance?

A n amazing dancer gives 100% effort!

N o, modern is not slow... It's very quick!

C an you gracefully drop down into the splits?

E xcitement spreads through the audience.

Isabel Duffy (7)

I'm Mia Rose, The Unknown

I solated is how I feel at lunchtime when I'm sitting all alone

M y life is littered with the most perfect people

M ystery is why

I solation at school is like missing out on everything

A rt is where I'm not trapped

R ose petals on the ground, around all the couples

O f course, I'm alone, not one friend

S oft, delicate butterflies crowd the pretty girls

E verything and everyone is there.

Mia King (11)

Creative

C lumsy; I often fall over my own feet!

R eading stories before bedtime is exciting.

E ating picnics and lots of yummy foods at restaurants is lots of fun!

A rty things like drawing, painting and modelling are my favourite.

T rying my best is important, even when I am not very good at something.

I magining I am a doctor helps me practise for when I'm older.

V aluable to my friends and family.

E xcited about surprises!

Eve Greenoak (6)

Joyous To Be Me

I ntelligent, yes, I don't like to boast

S erious, but silly, maybe more than most

O ptimistic towards an open opportunity

B rightly shining, with a smile that brings unity

E nthusiastic, eager to develop and explore whilst

L oving those around me and more!

R eading is a daily activity

I always have a spark of creativity

C urious, always love a debate

H appy that I am Isobel and great!

Isobel Rich (10)

My Personality

P assionate about life

E nergetic all through the day

R eaching for the stars

S ports are what I love: cricket, football and swimming

O pen to trying new things

N utritious food is good for me

A dventurous when I'm outdoors

L ean and strong, running along

I ntrigued by other life in space

T ranquil music is what I make

Y earning to read every book in the world!

Arhan Aul (7)

Benjamin

B orn in Sutton Coldfield on the 7th October, 2014

E ight is my number at Sutton United FC

N erf guns are my favourite game

J ungle gym in my garden is where I love to climb

A lfie is my older brother and football-mad too

M usic is always on in our house and I play the guitar

I want to be a builder and Grandad has given me his tools

N ow I'm off to play with my friends at Coppice School.

Benjamin Passey (7)

Big Brother

B eing a big brother is the best
I love it so much
G rab the poopy nappies and put them in the bin!

B ath time with him is my favourite
R eading with my brother is fun
O ne, two, three - I teach him numbers
T ickling my brother is amazing
H e does the sweetest giggles
E very night, I give him a goodnight kiss
R emembering all the good times makes me feel happy.

Jasper Tinmurth (7)

Dinosaurs

D inosaurs are all different

I nside their bodies are 852 bones

N yontosaurus had over 10,000 teeth

O range, green and brown are some of the colours

S uchomimus used to eat meat and fish

A nkylosaurus had spikes to protect itself

U raltosaurus was a carnivore

R ugops was longer than a whale shark

S aurophaganax was stronger than a T-rex, strong enough to kill a T-rex too.

Muhammed Khizar Khan (7)

Nature Walks

N umber of trees
A nimals are extraordinary and rare
T rees with apples on them
U nleashed animals so happy and free
R ainforests are damp like a shallow pond
E nter the forest

W onders to see
A nts crawling on the ground
L ovely sights to see
K estrels flying around in a circle
S ticks and twigs on the ground.

Prisha Jain (9)

Become Greater

M agic maths
U seful to know
L imitless counting
T imes tables
I nteresting timesing
P ositioning numbers
L essons in class
I love maths
C onquering it
A nybody can try it
T hree times tables
I nvestigating numbers
O dd and even
N obody should give up!

Oliver Smith (7)

All About Me

E xcellent brown hair and very pretty face
V ery cool like ice cream on a hot day
A mazing at listening and very kind

J oyful with friends
O nly like lasagne, it's my favourite
R espectful to my brother and Mum
D o well in music and at school
A wesome at gymnastics
N ice to others.

Eva Jordan (7)

All About Me

H umorous stories about giraffes make me smile

A giraffe is my favourite animal because they are kind and fast

R unning is what I like to do sometimes

R ainbows I like to take pictures of

I like to be imaginative

E nthusiastic about writing which makes me happy

T hese are some of my favourite things to do!

Harriet Lodge

Rainbows

R ainbows come on rainy days
A ll the colours you could imagine
I n the dark, you cannot see a rainbow
N ever in your lives will it be a dull moment when you see a rainbow
B right and beautiful
O ne pot of gold at the end
W hen will the rainbow end?
S o what a beautiful sight they are to see.

Megan Jones (6)

Isabella

I ntelligent brain buzzing all day

S pecial girl, friendly and kind

A rty and crafty, loves messy play

B oujee and stylish, fashion on my mind

E verything fast, run, run, run!

L oves sugar, mainly pancakes

L ots of energy! Running is fun!

A lways moving from the moment I wake.

Isabella Loughlin (5)

Rishay

R eal superheroes are kind and caring

I see them everywhere - mostly without capes

S howing up with kind words and a helping hand

"H ey, do you want to play with me?" I ask when I see someone who is lonely

A lways willing to share, to show that I care

Y es, I am a superhero too.

Rishay Ashwin (6)

I Am Keen

M y mind is amazing because I am really good at maths

I am amazing because I do everything my mum says

L ovely words really are important to me

L oyalty is very important because it is a very good skill

E xcellent is being very good at what you do

R adiant sunshine is great to see.

Miller Lewis (7)

This Is My Life

L ovely, funny, dark hair is my style and dodgy peach skin

E njoy eating fruit and vegetables, what a healthy diet I have!

W orry if I get something wrong

I 'm great at my favourite sports: snooker and football

S pectacular at drawing and reading. My favourite books are Horrid Henry.

Lewis Emery (6)

This Is Fintan

F riendly in everything I do

I ntelligent and enthusiastic at maths and TT Rock Stars

N ever gives up at any sport, even if you suck, you will learn

T alented, can play football, basketball and rugby

A nimal-loving nerd

N ever give up being me, even when things are tough.

Fintan Riley (10)

All About Me

E verything about me

L izey is my nickname

I like pizza

Z ebras are on my water bottle

A thing I like doing is junk modelling

B eano is my favourite magazine

E lsie is my cousin

T ree climbing is great

H ave you found out about me?

Elizabeth Hatt (6)

The Life Of Vikram

V ictory is the sweetest taste you can get

I love bubblegum ice cream

K arate lessons are my favourite thing to do

R acing and running are my favourite things to do

A rsenal are my second favourite team in the league

M artin Ødegaard is my favourite player.

Vikram Singh

Fantastic Football

F eet kicking around the ball
O utstanding goals every second
O utrageous chants
T elevisions being watched by football fans
B all shooting into the goal
A lmighty goals and strong tackles
L ong pass and...
L iverpool score against Newcastle.

Arihaan Anand (6)

Kindness

K indness matters to me

I t is who I am

N ice words are good to hear

D oing good does you good

N ever go without a 'Hello, how are you?'

E veryone deserves it

S o let us do it!

S tay calm and show kindness... That is how I do it.

Lydia Eleftheriades (5)

Elodie

E nergetic, fun, kind sister

L eopard Girl is my superhero name

O aty bars, chocolate and tomatoes are my favourite foods

D rawing and swinging are my favourite things to do

I look after nature every single day

E lodie is my name and I like blue and pink.

Elodie Reed (6)

Hallie Blake

H appy all the time
A rtistic and creative
L ikes slime
L oves my cat, Jake
I dol is my mum
E njoy nature and animals

B ravery
L oves school
A good football player
K een writer
E ducational.

Hallie Blake (9)

Michole

M oxie is my dog, I love her very much

I like the colour green

C hocolate is my favourite snack

H elpful is what my parents often say about me

O range is my favourite fruit

L ovely is my smile

E xcellent is what I get for my hard work.

Michole Opoku Agyeman (7)

I Love Dinosaurs

D inosaurs lived long ago
I think dinosaurs are great
N o dinosaurs exist today
O ne type of dinosaur is a T-rex
S ome dinosaurs swim
A dinosaur likes to eat
U nder the ground are fossils
R are fossils are in museums.

Holly White (6)

This Is Me - Joshion

J ovial and jolly little me
O ften outspoken but
S ensitive and sincere to my friends
H igh-spirited, humble and happy little me
I mpressing everyone with my imaginative and
O utstanding Lego builds
N ice but noisy little meeeee!

Joshion Philip Sajith Arattu (5)

My Dreams

"D o you have any dreams, dear bear?"

"R eally, you want pink fur?

E ating all the juicy pears?"

"A ll of them are dreams," said other bears.

"M y dreams are my funfairs.

S ee you later, my dears!"

Suendam Cakir (6)

All About Me!

A new toy to play with and I hope it's exciting!

L ots of special love just for me

I like strawberry ice cream but only in the summer

C an I go out with my friend because I'm bored?

E nthusiastic about everything I do and I love to learn.

Alice Thompson (6)

Sports Of Me

T he dream is my heart

E verything in my mind is sports

N ever give up on whatever you do

N ever just never give up on your dream

I f you give up on sports or music, I will not be happy

S o please don't give up, please, can you not?

Georgie Franklin (7)

All About Me

E nergetic sports are very good for me
M y mind is so good, so I can think
I 'm kind to my friends
L oyal friends of mine are kind
I 'm thankful for my family because they give me lots of presents
E lephants are my favourite.

Emilie Paul (7)

Gift's Amazing Acrostic Poem About School

S pectacular caterpillar turned into a butterfly

C urious frog leapt into the pond

H appy monkey liked the banana

O utstanding rabbit ate so many carrots

O rganised birds keep their nest tidy

L ovely puppy ate all the dog food.

Gift Ogundipe (5)

Noor

N ani's house is my favourite place to be

O utdoors is where I like to spend my time, especially on woodland walks

O wls are a type of bird I learnt about in my home-school

R eading stories to my baby sister and brothers is something I enjoy.

Noor-ul-faatiha Mahmood (6)

All About Me

O h my, what a star I am!

S o strong and brave, but pretty scared of the dark

C areful with other people, but sometimes a little rough

A nimals are my favourite things, especially rabbits

R C cars are one of my favourite things.

Oscar Pyatt (7)

This Is Me

E very day, I like to meet my friends

L ovely is my teddy and she is cuddly

S uper pizza for my tea and sometimes for my lunch

I am a kind friend at Coppice Primary School

E nergetic jogging is very good for me and my family.

Elsie Terry (7)

This Is Me

A wesome

I ncredible

N urturing

S uperb

L yrical

E xtraordinary

Y outhful

T errific

S uperhero

A mbitious

N oble

G rateful

A ngel.

Ainsley Tsanga

My Life

P erfect at being the captain of my football team

A nd enjoying every minute of this new theme

V ery kind and very fair is the only way to be

A s happy as can be, just like a dream

N ice and helpful like a splashing stream.

Pavan Briah (7)

Easter

E ggs made of chocolate
A sh Wednesday is the state of Lent
S unday services about Easter happen
T hree days later, Jesus rose again
E aster bunny gives us chocolate eggs
R ejoice, everyone! It is Easter!

Reward Agbaje (7)

Edith

E dith is amazing in lots of different ways

D eep in Edith's heart, she loves and cares for others

I am a kind and generous person

T he family she lives with are kind like her

H er heart is a piece of gold.

Edith Shepherd (6)

All About Me

I am very kind

M y hair is blackish brown and my eyes are brown

O h, how I love going to school!

G reat is how I feel when I swim

E very day, I do pictures for fun

N ow I can write an acrostic poem.

Imogen Plummer (6)

Temple

T iger is climbing up a tree
E lephant is drinking a cup of tea
M onkey is playing hide-and-seek
P anther is going at a fast speed
L eopard is counting one, two, three
E agle swoops around the tree.

David Davies (6)

Rocket

R acing through space

O pposing gravity

C reative engineers plan the build

K rushnic Effect is when the rocket makes lots of noise but doesn't go anywhere!

E xtreme power

T ime to blast off!

Riley Seaton (9)

Animals

A nimals are amazing

N ewts are amphibians

I guanas have sharp claws

M onkeys swing in trees

A ntelope live in herds

L ions, leopards, cheetahs

S o many more to discover.

Ethan Boyle (5)

Things That Make Me, Me

T alented at acro dance

H ave a dog

I love pandas

S wim every Saturday

I am a cheerleader

S cience expert

M osaic artist

E xpert at geography.

Ilinca Maria Istrati (10)

My World

C ousins care for me and my brother
H elpful and tidies the classroom when it is messy
L oves Barbies, swimming and gymnastics
O pen at school and very kind
E xcellent at loads of subjects.

Chloe Higgins (6)

Stanley

S ausages are my favourite thing to eat
T hey are really tasty
A nd I love them! I also love
N ectarines. They are
L ovely
E specially when they are juicy and
Y ummy!

Stanley Clark (7)

All About Me

M arvellous blue eyes
Y ou're a star too
S ometimes I can go on my Switch
E nthusiastic and funny is what you'll get
L ove playing Chicken Run
F antastic and fabulous.

James Jordan (7)

Excited About Nature

E ggs hatching

X -ray fish swimming

C ats purring

I guanas camouflaging

T igers roaring

E lephants squirting

D id you know, nature makes me feel excited?!

Melissa Roberts (6)

This Is Me: Amreet

A fantastic friend!
M y best friend is my daddy
R eally love to eat sushi
E veryone thinks I am funny
E xcellent reader, says my teacher
T his is me, I am Amreet.

Amreet Kaur Bhogal (6)

Diya

D octors are kind, loving and helpful

I 'm going to become a doctor in the future

Y ou are going to be my patient

A lways, I will be quick and alert in the case of an emergency.

Diya Kakollu (7)

This Is Me

A leena is my name
L ovely to everyone around me
E xcellent at gymnastics
E xtraordinary in every way
N ature exploring is my favourite
A nd this is me.

Aleena Noor (7)

Brave

B e brave and courageous
R eady to help others
A ll the people should live in peace
V ery hard-working boy I am
E veryone should respect one another.

Rikhil Kakollu (5)

Happy

H elping others makes me happy
A nd looking at my favourite things
P laying with my BFFs
P lanning things that are nearby
Y ummy apples in my tummy.

Nell McCulloch (7)

I Like Ice Cream!

I nteresting
C runchy
E xciting

C omestible
R unny
E njoyable
A ppetising
M arshmallow-flavoured ice cream!

Alveen Muhammad

Trains

T rains are tremendously strong
R acing like a rocket
A lways on time
I gnite the firebox!
N oisy whistle
S treamlined trains are fast!

Noah Seaton (9)

Meet Nathen

N ice but noisy

A wesome and amazing

T errific at tennis and football

H appy and hungry

E nergetic and encouraging

N aturally nimble.

Nathen Dineth Tibenderana (8)

All About Me!

H appy go lucky chappy
A lways looking for an adventure
R eally funny and cheeky
R eliable and loyal
Y ou won't find anyone else like me!

Harry Demetriou (8)

My Name

Z ayn is my name
A wesome is what I am
"Y ahoo!" is what I yell when I'm having fun
N ever is it boring when I'm around!

Zayn Hussain (7)

This Is Me

G aming is cool
A mazing is what I am
M inecraft is the future world
E very day, I play games
R oblox has so many games.

Vishnu Vinodh

Malik

M agnificent boy

A rt is fun

L oves the Xbox

I ntelligence is my thing

K angaroos are one of my favourite animals.

Malik Baillie (6)

Bubba

B ubbas are my favourite teddies
U sually in my bed
B eside me when I was a baby
B eside me now
A lways with me.

Evie Kennedy (7)

My World

E xcellent at rock climbing
D ecorating things in my house
I ce skating is my favourite thing
E verything makes me laugh.

Edie Vinall (7)

Happy

H aving fun
A mazing things to do
P laying on my iPad
P laying with my friends
Y ears of your lifetime.

Yahya Afify (7)

Friendship

E verybody can be my friend
V ery good friends are important
I am at an amazing school
E verybody is my friend.

Evie Clewer (6)

My Hobby

M elodious
U pbeat to dance
S oft, smooth and soothing
I nstrumental
C lassical and choral.

Sivataruniya Piratheepan

Pugs

P aws are medium-sized
U nique in nature
G orgeous and remarkable
S uper cute dogs.

Rejoice Agbaje (7)

All About Alfie

T his is me, a tiny bit small
H appy most of the time
I love my brother, my mum and my dad
S o excited to ride my bike

I play nicely with my brother
S o nicely till it is teatime

M y brother is really kind, so we have fun
when we play
E very day we play together, I don't want
him to go away.

This is me.

Alfie Sanderson (7)
Hunwick Primary School, Hunwick

Hi, I'm Masie

T his is me, Masie

H i, I am 6 years old

I love my mum, my dad, Chloe, Ellie and my little dog too

S illy Alfie the dog sometimes trips us over and jumps on us

I really like school, my favourite part is learning

S ophie is my friend and I play with everyone too!

M asie is my name

E very day, I am happy.

Masie Griffiths (6)
Hunwick Primary School, Hunwick

Happy Beatrice

T he nature is my favourite to see
H appy and cheerful it is
I really like rainbows, they are so lovely
S miley and kind is what I am

I like playing outside
S ometimes I go dancing, it is really fun

M y sister is always happy
E xtremely good and kind.

Hi, my name is Beatrice, this is me.

Beatrice Barker (7)
Hunwick Primary School, Hunwick

Rainbow Panda

T his is me

H appy and cheerful

I love cats, rainbows and pandas

S miley and proud

I love to sew

S ometimes I play with my cat, Big Spit

M e and my friends like playing

E very day, I love rainbow pandas.

This is me.

Sienna Blacklock (7)

Hunwick Primary School, Hunwick

All About Aimee

T iny and happy
H appy and helpful
I love my brother
S o excited and cheerful

I am seven
S miling at everyone

M y family is the best
E veryone is my friend, I am kind to everyone.

Everyone, this is me.

Aimee Reidy (7)
Hunwick Primary School, Hunwick

Hi, I Am Theo

T his is me

H i, I am Theo

I love football

S ometimes I am really happy

I like walking

S ometimes I feel great

M y brother is cute

E very day, I am smiling.

Hi, I am Theo and this is me.

Theo Cottrell (7)
Hunwick Primary School, Hunwick

All About Me

T his is me

H appy and kind

I love horse riding

S ad and happy sometimes

I like playing with Liberty

S ometimes I play with Eva

M y name is Jessica

E lephants make me happy!

Jessica Fielding (6)
Hunwick Primary School, Hunwick

This Is Me

T he first thing people think of me is that I'm ordinary, but if you take a closer look, I am extraordinary. Why would I be someone else when I can be me? I love my brother and sister, but beware, they can be deadly!

H appy, sad, angry or calm, keep these emotions so they are safe from harm. Fast and enthusiastic, amazing as can be, everyone has different traits, I can guarantee.

I love music, it has nice beats, people like different things as I can see. I like very vibrant colours as they are admirable. Why should we be the same if we can have our own style?

S ome work slow, some are efficient, but we all know that we are different. We are all unique in a way, and if we weren't? Well, Earth would be boring because we'd all be the same.

I am crazy, wacky, weird and fun. I like football and love to run. I am good at art and models too. I am very kind and very true. My favourite animal is a panda that is cuddly and cute. Their favourite food is bamboo.

S emih is my noble name that has caught lots of fame. My super style is breathtakingly cool but all of this is very new.

M y hobby is looking for treasure, this might carry on forever and ever. I play outside quite a lot. If you relax, your worries will be forgotten.

E arth is a very nice place and I feel comfy in this place. I still have a future way beyond that I can write in any font.

This is me.

Semih Quoi (9)
Sherfield School, Sherfield-On-Loddon

This Is Me!

B rodie likes basketball

A lways playing with my friends

S hooting the ball into the hoop

K ilograms, the ball weighs

E verybody trying to get better

T he ball is easy to get the hang of

B rothers can play it too

A n amazing sport to play

L eaving basketball makes me sad

L earning skills every week!

Brodie Miller (7)

St Bride's Primary School, Bothwell

This Is Me!

G abriella is my name
A balloon is my favourite
B right and colourful eyes I have
R ed is my favourite colour
I play with my iPad
E lectronics are my thing
L ove is my favourite
L ovely me
A rainbow makes me happy!

Gabriella Canale (7)
St Bride's Primary School, Bothwell

This Is Me!

N ew York is a great place

E veryone rushing to go places

W andering around lots of shops

Y ummy pizza for my dinner

O h look, there's the Statue of Liberty

R hinos in the zoo

K eeping busy on my holiday in New York.

Michael McCann (8)

St Bride's Primary School, Bothwell

This Is Me!

P laying with my friends at school
L aughing with my sister at home
A sking my mum and dad for toys
Y o-yos are one of my favourite toys
I n my room, playing with my dog
N ever ever mean to anyone
G reen is my favourite colour.

Jack Reid (7)
St Bride's Primary School, Bothwell

This Is Me!

S carpering up trees

Q uick climber

U p a tree, eating nuts

I ntelligent little creatures

R eally small and cute

R ummaging through the crunchy leaves

E xcellent at hiding from us

L ong, soft tail.

Matthew Donnelly (7)
St Bride's Primary School, Bothwell

This Is Me

M y favourite colour is green
I like football
C heese is my least favourite
H appy as can be
A nimals like tigers amaze me
E veryone thinks I'm funny
L ittle animals are not my thing.

Michael McCallum (7)
St Bride's Primary School, Bothwell

This Is Me!

M y favourite animal is a monkey

O ther people are nice to me

N o monkey is mean

K ites are what I like to play with

E veryone is friends with me

Y es, this is my favourite animal.

Ezmay Dooley (7)
St Bride's Primary School, Bothwell

This Is Me!

M onty is the best pet in the world
O n the tablet, I always draw him
N o fear, yes, he has no fear
T he best fish friend I could ask for
Y es, the best pet in the world!

Alexander Farr (7)
St Bride's Primary School, Bothwell

This Is Me!

E lements as beautiful as me

I love my family

L earning things every day

I love food

D efinitely funny

H elpful every day.

Eilidh Scott (7)
St Bride's Primary School, Bothwell

My Favourite Colour

B lue is my favourite colour
L ovely, bright blue sky
U nique and interesting shades of blue
E verybody likes blue.

James Reddin
St Bride's Primary School, Bothwell

This Is Me!

B rave

R esponsible

O range is my favourite colour

O utstanding

K ind

E ating is my jam!

Brooke McManus (7)
St Bride's Primary School, Bothwell

My Pet

B lack is his colour

E veryone thinks he is cute

"N o!" is what we say to him all the time.

Lochlan Taggart (7)
St Bride's Primary School, Bothwell

This Is Me!

D ogs are fun
O range is the colour of the sun
G oing for a walk with my dog.

Antonia Moraru (7)
St Bride's Primary School, Bothwell

This Is Me!

M y name is Mia
I love horses
A mazing, beautiful, strong animals.

Mia Craney (7)

St Bride's Primary School, Bothwell

Kindness

K ind
I listen to others who look after you
N ever give up
D o safe games
N ever say unkind words
E ach other give respect
S ay happy birthday to you
S how respect, stand up for yourself.

Lilly-Rose Holdsworth (7)
Summerfield Primary School, Leeds

Kindness

K ind and caring

I can tell you things

N ever be unkind

D on't hurt me

N ot being a bully

E ach of us has fun

S ay happy birthday

S itting with my friends.

Casey (7)
Summerfield Primary School, Leeds

Kindness

K ind, super person
I can understand you
N ice, super friend
D oesn't push me
N ice listener
E xcellent helper
S kip together
S how respect.

Nathan Grabowski (6)
Summerfield Primary School, Leeds

Kindness

K ind to each other
I ndividual friends
N ice to my friends
D o kind things
N ever be a bully
E ach of us has fun
S how respect
S tand up for you.

Poppy (6)
Summerfield Primary School, Leeds

Honesty

H ave fun

O n their feet

N ow we have fun

E ach of us has fun

S hare your cake

T ell you things

Y ou are the best person in the world.

Travis Hannah (7)

Summerfield Primary School, Leeds

Caring

C elebrate my birthday
A re you my friend?
R un
I look after you
N ice and be kind
G ood listener.

Junior (7)
Summerfield Primary School, Leeds

My Brother, George

G reen is his favourite colour
E nergetic and lively
O utstanding brother
R acket is his favourite game
G rass, he likes lying in it
E lephants are his favourite animal.

Kasey Wilson (7)
Topcliffe Primary School, Birmingham

My Favourite Animal

S harks like hunting
H unting juicy fish
A baby shark is harmless
R oaming waters, looking for fish
K illing machines!

Kyce Isaac-Witts (7)

Topcliffe Primary School, Birmingham

My Favourite Animal

F luffy

L azy

A mazing

M arvellous

I ncredible

N ice

G reat

O utstanding.

Georgia Shearer (7)

Topcliffe Primary School, Birmingham

My Friend, Poppy

P oppy loves elephants
O utstanding friend
P oppy loves macaroons
P oppy loves the beach
Y ear 3 besties.

Summer Hope (7)

Topcliffe Primary School, Birmingham

My Teacher, Miss Halford

H appy

A mazing

L ovely

F riendly

O utstanding

R ole model

D elightful.

Daisy Pritchard (7)

Topcliffe Primary School, Birmingham

Me

N ever mean
O utstanding friend
A mazing at sports
H ealthy helper.

Noah Antcliff (7)

Topcliffe Primary School, Birmingham

My Spare Time!

S leeping

P laying

A rt

R eading

E ating.

Katie-Rose Griffiths (8)

Topcliffe Primary School, Birmingham

My Name

J olly
A mazing
C ool
K ind.

Jack Ancill-Durham (7)

Topcliffe Primary School, Birmingham

Ruby, My Dog

R uby pounces on spiders
U nusually excellent at cuddles
B est at fetching a ball
Y ellowy, gingery brown fur

M ummy loves her
Y ummy dog treats are her favourite

D efinitely the best dog in the world
O utside, she plays with her ball
G reat at cheering me up.

Harrison-J Odell (6)
Totternhoe CE Academy, Totternhoe

Spider-Man

S pidey is cool

P owerful webs from his hands

I n his powers, he has webs

D ay and night, he fights villains

E xcellent at saving the world

R eally exciting when he saves the day

M arvellous at being a hero

A vengers he is part of

N ever be rude to Spider-Man.

Ethan Tingay (7)
Totternhoe CE Academy, Totternhoe

Football

F ootball is fantastic

O nce scored four goals in one game

O nly score good goals

T ierney is one of my favourite footballers

B runo Fernandes is epic

A rsenal are one of the best teams in the world

L ionel Messi is one of my favourites

L acazette is amazing.

Alden Rust (7)
Totternhoe CE Academy, Totternhoe

My Family

M ummy is in charge of my family
Y ou are lovely

F amilies are nice
A mazing family
M y family is very nice to me
I am very kind to my family
L ovely families
Y ou have a lovely family.

Poppy Tebbutt (6)
Totternhoe CE Academy, Totternhoe

Twinkle

T he star is shining every night

W hen the star twinkles

I like stars

N ight-night

K now that they will always sparkle

L ight and magic are what they give

E very night, stars shine.

Olivia Noble (6)
Totternhoe CE Academy, Totternhoe

Ionatan

I am Ionatan

O range chocolate is the best

N ature is my favourite thing

A lways laughing

T omorrow, my uncle is coming

A lways playing with my train tracks

N ever tells lies.

Ionatan Patrichi (6)

Totternhoe CE Academy, Totternhoe

Cupcake

C akes are yummy

U nbelievably tasty

P udding is the best

C akes are unhealthy

A lways cupcakes

K imberley loves cupcakes too

E very day, I love to eat cupcakes.

Martha Setterfield (7)

Totternhoe CE Academy, Totternhoe

Otto M C

O tto is a very rare name
T he people are not perfect
T hey are very emotional
O tto is my favourite name

M y brother is mischievous

C larke is not rare.

Otto Clarke (6)
Totternhoe CE Academy, Totternhoe

School

S uper at reading and writing

C ool at swimming

H appy and enjoying maths

O range is a colour in the rainbow

O ranges are my favourite fruit

L earning is amazing.

Jessica Janes (6)
Totternhoe CE Academy, Totternhoe

Joshua

J igsaws are my favourite games
O ctopuses are cool
S and is fun to play with
H appiest when Meghan hugs me
U nbelievably tasty banana cake
A pples are yummy.

Joshua Law (6)
Totternhoe CE Academy, Totternhoe

Harry

H appiest person alive

A super gamer

R onaldo is my second favourite footballer

R eady to play football

Y ay, it's time to game.

Harry Shuffleton (6)
Totternhoe CE Academy, Totternhoe

Mummy

M y mummy is making cakes
U nbelievable cakes
M y mummy likes flowers
M y mummy likes cakes too
Y ummy cakes from my mummy.

David Frampton (7)
Totternhoe CE Academy, Totternhoe

Fairy

F airies are pretty

A t night, they come out

I n the dark, they glow

R ue loves them

Y ellow is their favourite colour.

Rue Smith (6)

Totternhoe CE Academy, Totternhoe

Bethany

B rave
E nthusiastic
T hankful
H appy
A lways joyful
N ever unkind
Y ou are fantastic.

Bethany Phillips (5)
Totternhoe CE Academy, Totternhoe

Charlie

C aring

H andsome

A lways sweet

R eally kind

L ovely

I nteresting

E nthusiastic.

Charlie Chandler (6)
Totternhoe CE Academy, Totternhoe

Oliver

O verly caring

L oving

I nviting

V ery nice to my friends

E ntertaining

R eally funny.

Oliver Mumford (5)

Totternhoe CE Academy, Totternhoe

Evelyn

E xcellent

V ery helpful

E nthusiastic

L ovely

Y ou are the best

N ever unkind.

Evelyn Absalom (6)

Totternhoe CE Academy, Totternhoe

Reggie

R eally kind

E xciting

G reat ideas

G ood listener

I nteresting

E nthusiastic.

Reggie Coppock (6)

Totternhoe CE Academy, Totternhoe

Seren

S o wonderful

E xciting

R eally happy

E ntertaining

N ever unkind.

Seren Low (5)

Totternhoe CE Academy, Totternhoe

Taiya

T alented
A mazing
I nteresting
Y ou are funny
A lways brave.

Taiya Douglas (6)
Totternhoe CE Academy, Totternhoe

Caleb

C ool
A mazing
L ovely friend
E xciting
B rilliant.

Caleb Derbidge (6)

Totternhoe CE Academy, Totternhoe

Enzo

E nthusiastic
N ever unkind
Z estful
O verly happy.

Enzo Apollonio (6)

Totternhoe CE Academy, Totternhoe

Luis

L ovely
U nique
I nteresting
S uper.

Luis Cox (6)
Totternhoe CE Academy, Totternhoe

Young Writers Information

We hope you have enjoyed reading this book – and that you will continue to in the coming years.

If you're the parent or family member of an enthusiastic poet or story writer, do visit
www.youngwriters.co.uk/subscribe
and sign up to receive news, competitions, writing challenges and tips, activities and much, much more! There's lots to keep budding writers motivated!

If you would like to order further copies of this book, or any of our other titles, then please give us a call or order via your online account.

Young Writers
Remus House
Coltsfoot Drive
Peterborough
PE2 9BF
(01733) 890066
info@youngwriters.co.uk

Join in the conversation!
Tips, news, giveaways and much more!

f YoungWritersUK **𝕏** YoungWritersCW **◎** youngwriterscw